Sorry To Hear About Your Hamster

By: Colleen Hollis

Illustrated and digitized by Colleen Hollis
Copyright © 2024 Colleen's Children Line Inc. Ltd.
Publisher: Colleen's Novels Inc. Ltd.
ISBN: 978-1-964768-16-8

I am so sorry to have heard about your beloved hamster

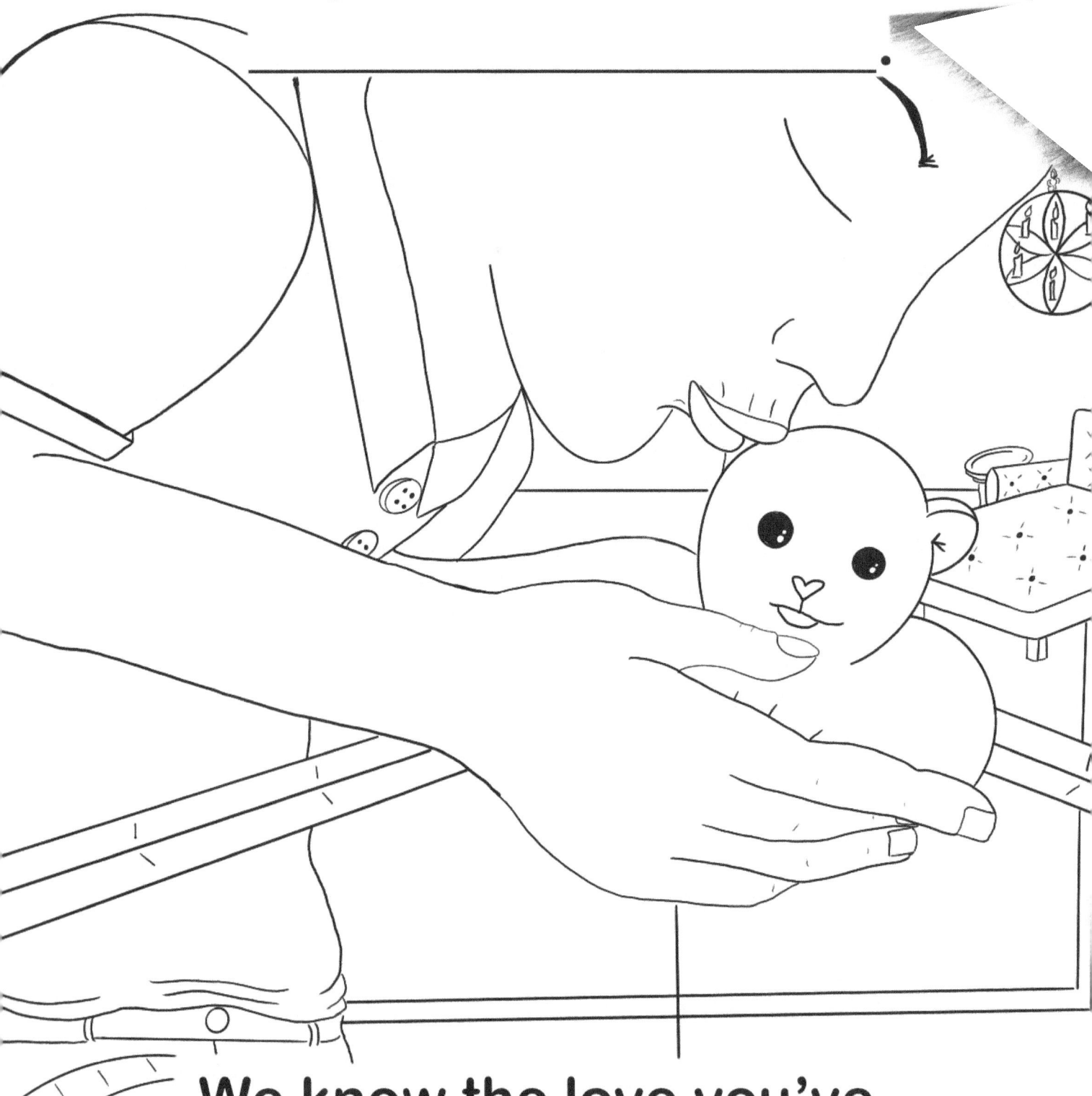

We know the love you've shared with your fur-ever friend has meant so much to you.

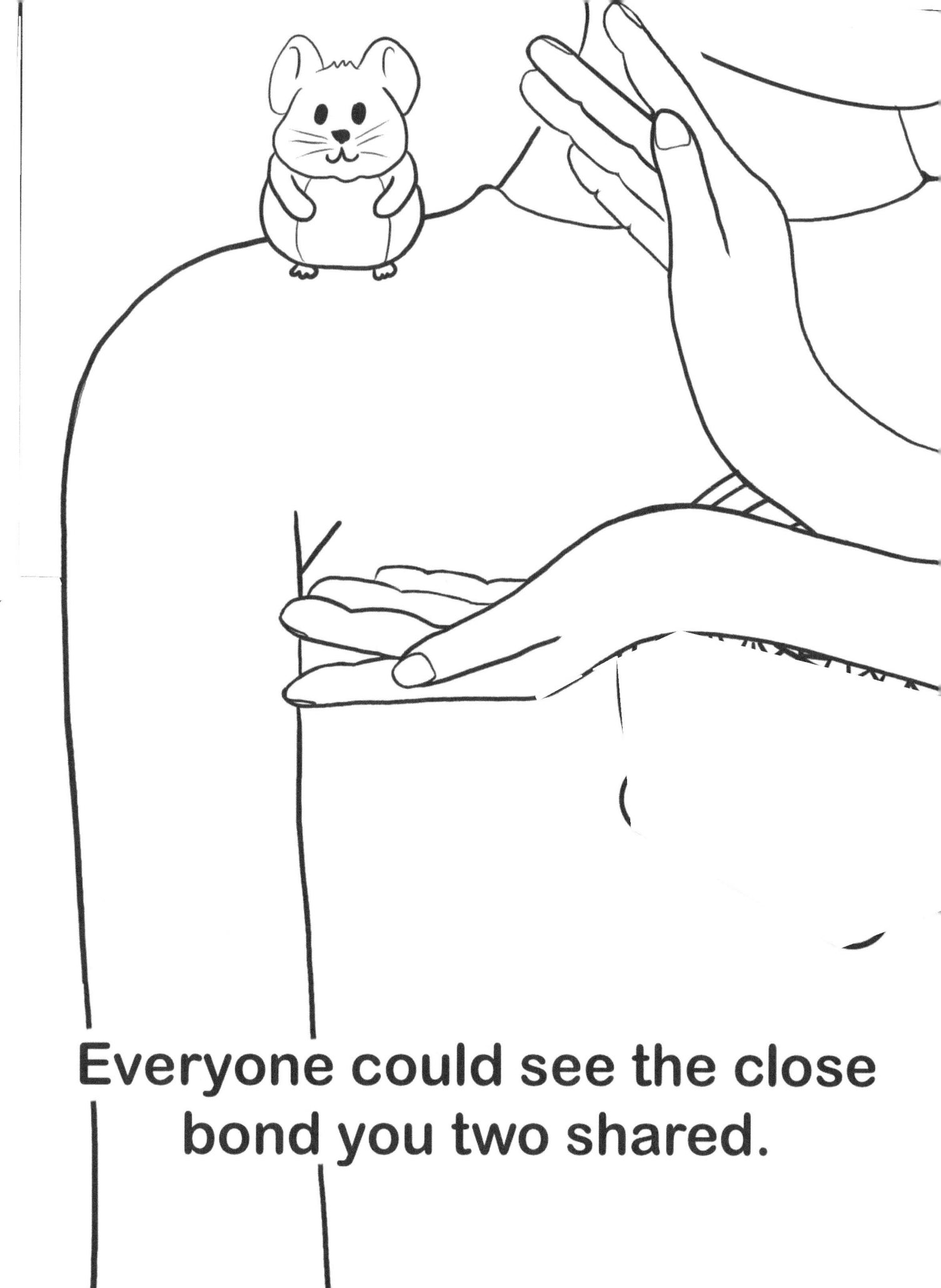

Everyone could see the close
bond you two shared.

We understand how much it hurts
to say goodbye to someone so dear.

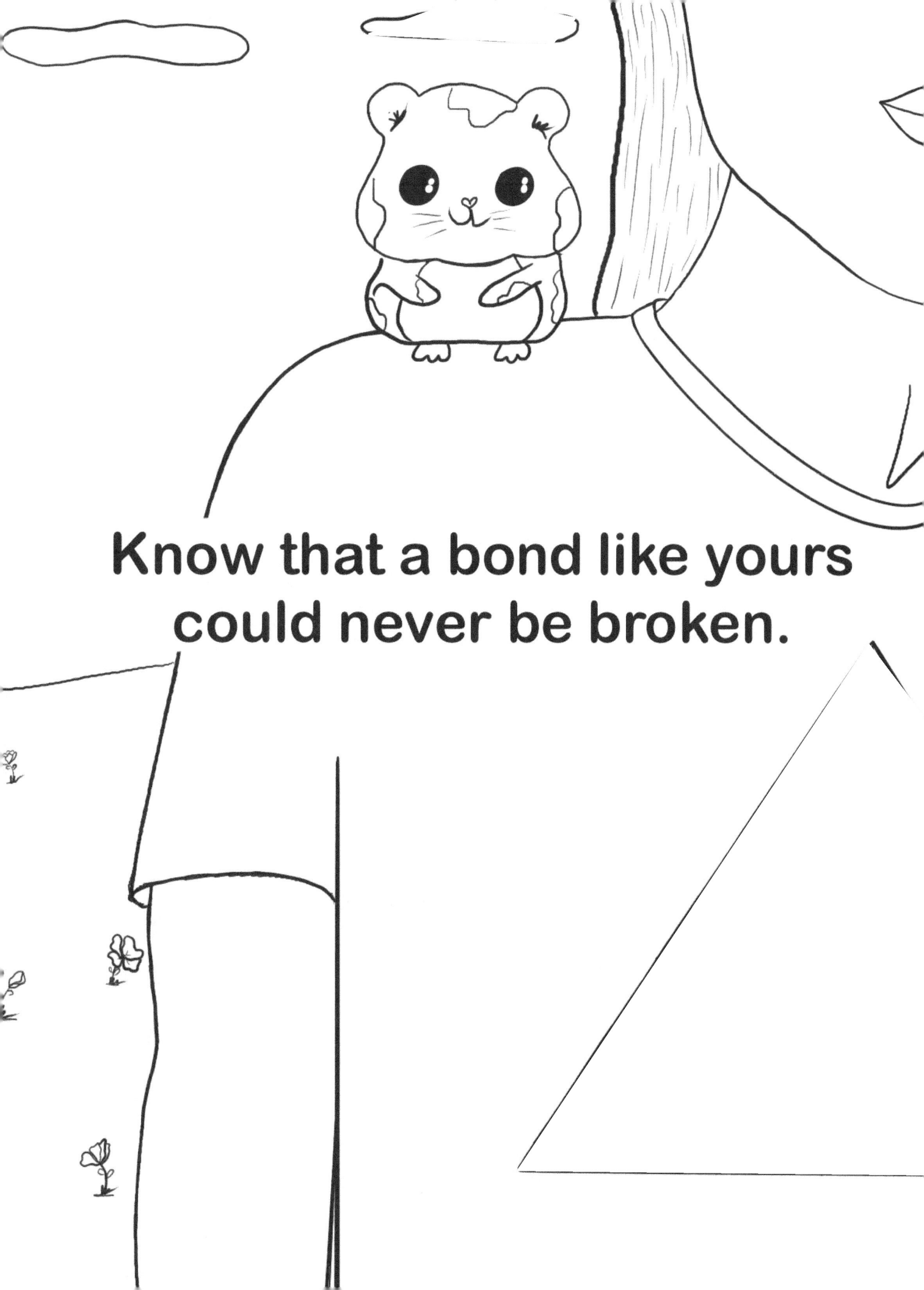

Know that a bond like yours
could never be broken.

Find comfort in thinking back to times that made you laugh.

...Like when your fur-friend would run so fast on it's wheel that it seemed like it was running a race we never knew about.

Or how it would do a front flip and appear to be dizzy when it would run too fast in it's ball.

Remember back to how during playtime it would cause all kinds of mischief throughout the house?

These silly moments will really help as time goes on.

The memories may bring tears
now, but with time the tears will
eventually turn into smiles.

It will help to recall all the time you spent together, and how much joy you brought to one another.

You did an awesome job being a friend to your pet.

Even when it wasn't always easy and fun.

You showed a level of maturity that has made us so proud.

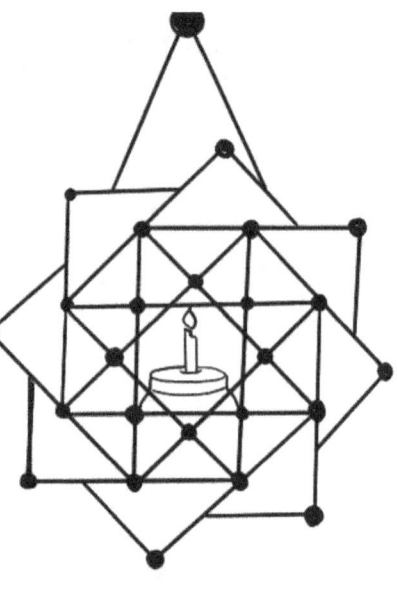

Please know you have support if you need any comforting.

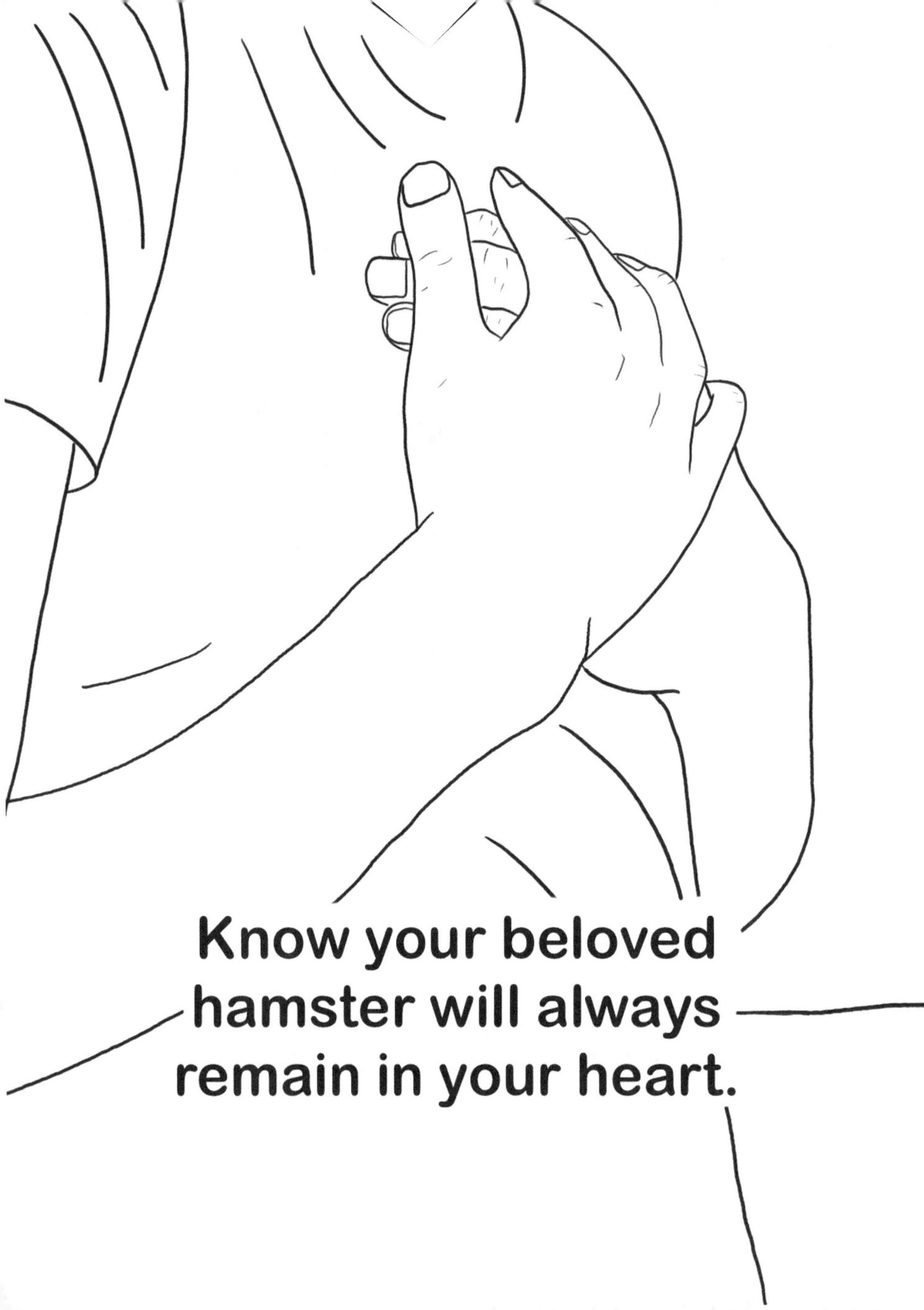

Know your beloved
hamster will always
remain in your heart.

If you need a shoulder to lean on while you cry, or just wish to have a friend to sit quietly with you when you feel down, I'm always here.

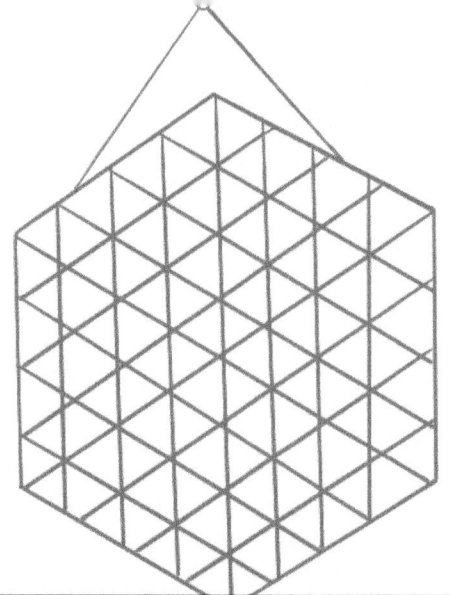

You are never dealing with this alone.

We're a team and we are always going to be there for each other.

Together we can get though this and anything else that comes our way.

We love you forever
and always.
Love, _____

Friend's Facts

Friend's Name:_____

Friend's Age:_____

Friend's Favorite Food/s:_____

_____

Friend's Favorite Activity:_____

_____

Friend's Favorite Toy/s: _____

_____

Friend's Favorite Person/s:_____

_____

Feel free to write a little note, or share a memory or two.

Sorry To Hear About Your Hamster, is one of the books in the children's line from Colleen's Bereavement Line For Children. Colleen's Bereavement Line for Children is aimed to assist in the healing process of children that find themselves navigating the loss of a loved one or pet. Sorry To Hear About Your Hamster focuses specifically on those with a hamster friend. A name can be added to the beginning of the book, while in the back of the book there is space to write memories about the fur-ever friend. Followed by a page for "Friend Facts" that can be filled in for a more personal feel.

All animal books in the series are interactive as well, they are in a coloring book format. Art has been shown as a useful tool that can aid in the healing process.

www.ingramcontent.com/pod-product-compliance
Lightning Source LLC
Chambersburg PA
CBHW081013120626

46546CB00010B/3140

9 781964 768168